Stop and Go, Yes and No

DIS

What Is an Antonym?

To my brother Kevin, who appreciates the richness of our language
—B.P.C.

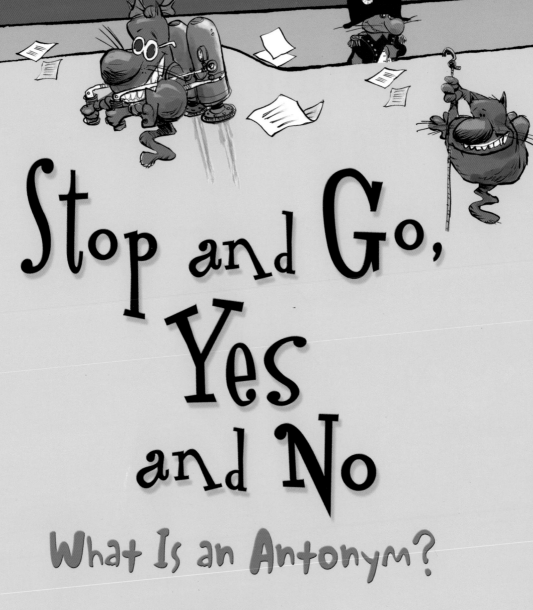

Stop and Go, Yes and No

What Is an Antonym?

by Brian P. Cleary

illustrated by Brian Gable

M MILLBROOK PRESS / MINNEAPOLIS

Antonyms are opposites— they're words like

stop and go.

See how different those words are?

They're just like yes and no.

Big and small are antonyms,
are antonyms,
and so are front and back,

fast
and
slow
and
high
and
low,
as well as white and black.

"I'd like to have
my chocolate hot,

'cause it's so cold today!"

Because of **antonyms**,
When things are right,
We'll say we're **glad**.

Like safe
compared to dangerous,

like heavy is to light,

shy to bold

and young to old

and even dim to bright,

They show a total contrast
just like
shamefully
and
proudly.

Sometimes **antonyms** are made with "un" before a word.

This is how we get unkind,

unable,

and unheard.

Often adding "dis"

or "im"

or sometimes even "non"

Will help you build an

antonym

with these beginnings on.

Antonyms help us divide

surrounded from alone.

And help compare the **famous**

to the totally **unknown**.

They point out lots of differences

like bald and extra hairy,

and give us words
to help us grow
a big Vocabulary.

Like hefty and diminutive,

absurd and somewhat normal.

Bravery and cowardice,

quite casual or formal.

In fall, the farmer
harvests crops.
In spring, he's busy
plantin' 'em.

So, what is an antonym?

ABOUT THE AUTHOR & ILLUSTRATOR

Brian P. Cleary is the author of the Words Are CATegorical©, Math Is CATegorical©, Adventures in Memory™, and Sounds Like Reading™ series. He has also written The Laugh Stand: Adventures in Humor; Peanut Butter and Jellyfishes: A Very Silly Alphabet Book; The Punctuation Station; and two poetry books. Mr. Cleary lives in Cleveland, Ohio.

Brian Gable is the illustrator of several Words Are CATegorical© books, as well as the Math Is CATegorical© series. Mr. Gable also works as a political cartoonist for the Globe and Mail newspaper in Toronto, Canada.

Millbrook Press
A division of Lerner Publishing Group, Inc.
241 First Avenue North
Minneapolis, MN 55401 USA

For reading levels and more information, look up this title at www.lernerbooks.com.

Library of Congress Cataloging-in-Publication Data

Cleary, Brian P., 1959—
    Stop and go, yes and no : what is an antonym? / by Brian P. Cleary ;
illustrations by Brian Gable.
    p.   cm. — (Words are categorical)
    ISBN 978—1—57505—860—3 (lib. bdg. : alk. paper)
    ISBN 978—0—8225—6535—2 (EB pdf)
    1. English language—Synonyms and antonyms—Juvenile literature. I. Gable,
Brian, 1949— ill. II. Title.
PE.1591.C563 2006
428.1—dc22   2005013391

Manufactured in China
10—41679—5456—3/23/2016